BEFORE YOU BEGIN...

Make sure to download the FREE audio program for this book which comes with your purchase! Just go to

www.slangman.com/audio

then look for your book and enter this code:

E2S2V9VTLJUL

GOLDILOCKS
and the 3 BEARS

Copy Editor: Julie Bobrick
Illustrated by: "Migs!" Sandoval
Translator: Marcela Redoles

Copyright © 2017 by David Burke

Email: info@heywordy.com
Website: www.heywordy.com

Hey Wordy! and all related characters and elements are © and trademarks of Hey Wordy, LLC.

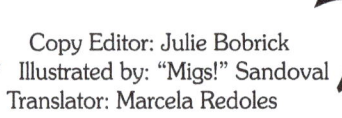

Published by Slangman Publishing. Slangman is a registered trademark of David Burke. All rights reserved. Reproduction or translation of any part of this work beyond that permitted by section 107 or 108 of the 1976 United States Copyright Act without the permission of the copyright owner is unlawful. Requests for permission or further information should be addressed to the Permissions Department, Slangman Publishing. This publication is designed to provide accurate and authoritative information in regard to the subject matter covered. The persons, entities and events in this book are fictitious. Any similarities with actual persons or entities, past and present, are purely coincidental.

ISBN13: 978-1-891888-28-1
Printed in the U.S.A.

Meet the Author
David Burke

Creator and star of the children's TV show, *Hey Wordy!*, David Burke has been single-handedly revolutionizing the foreign language-learning movement worldwide.

In addition to being a performer of boundless energy and enthusiasm, David speaks seven languages. A successful author and entrepreneur, he has built a thriving international publishing company featuring over 100 books he has written for teen/adults & children. His books have won publishing awards and have sold more than one million copies. David's Street Speak™ and Biz Speak™ series of books and audio programs are used around the world by government agencies, leading universities and major corporations.

Since age 4, David has been a classically trained pianist and uses his musical gifts to compose and perform original songs for his TV series, *Hey Wordy!* which introduces children to foreign languages and cultures through music, animation, and magical adventures. He has also composed, orchestrated, and performed all the music in the audio programs for each of these books.

David's engaging and charismatic persona became a fixture on broadcast entertainment channels around the world, such as CNN and the BBC. David and his work have been highlighted in many major publications, including The Los Angeles Times, The Chicago Tribune and The Christian Science Monitor.

"This series teaches everyday words that occur in your child's life, as well as terms having to do with politeness, greetings, family & friendship."

David Burke

Spanish vocabulary taught:

bebé = baby
blanda = soft
caliente = hot
cama = bed
cansada = tired
cocina = kitchen
tazón = bowl
dos = two
dura = hard
frío = cold

mamá = mama
mesa = table
oso = bear
papá = papa
paseo = stroll
pequeño = little
puerta = door
silla = chair
tres = three
uno = one

from Cindellera (Level 1)

adiós = goodbye
bonita = pretty
casa = house
de nada = you're welcome
enamorado = in love
esposa = wife
feliz = happy
fiesta = party
gracias = thank you
grande = big

guapo = handsome
mala = mean
medianoche = midnight
momento = moment
muchacha = girl
pie = foot
príncipe = prince
triste = sad
vestido = dress
zapato = shoe

1

oso

papá

mamá

Once upon a time, there was a bear family who lived in a *casa* in the forest — a papa oso, a mama who was very *bonita*, and their pride and joy, the cutest

baby oso. The **bebé oso** was very little. → **bebé**
→ **pequeño**
The **pequeño bebé oso** was also very
guapo like his **papá**. The **papá oso** was very
much *enamorado* with the **mamá** and they

were both very proud of their family. One day, the **mamá** prepared some soup for lunch, but it was too hot. While it cooled off, the **oso** family decided to go for a stroll.

paseo

Meanwhile in a town nearby, there lived a **muchacha** named Goldilocks who was very **bonita**, but also very **triste** because she never had anything fun to do.

5

She thought for a **momento** and came up with an idea. She decided to take a **paseo** in the forest. Very soon, she came upon a **casa** and knocked on the door but no one

puerta

was there. So she opened the **puerta**, put one *pie* inside the *casa*, and said "Hello? Is anyone home?" She was very tired after her long **paseo** and since no one answered,

cansada

mesa
cocina

she walked inside the *casa*. She looked around for a *momento* and was very *feliz* to see a table in the kitchen with food piled high on it!

Goldilocks quickly walked toward the **mesa** in the **cocina** and was super extra *feliz* because there on the **mesa** in the **cocina** was a bowl – **tazón**

uno
dos
tres

but not just (one), not just (two), but (three)! **Uno**, **dos**, **tres**! And the smell from each **tazón** was wonderful! So, she took a taste from the first **tazón** that belonged to

the **papá oso** and said, "This is too hot !" → **caliente**
Then she took a taste from the **tazón** that belonged to the **mamá** and said, "Oh! This is too cold !" Then she took a taste from → **frío**

the **tazón** of the **pequeño bebé oso** and said, "Ahhh. This one isn't too **caliente**. It isn't too **frío**. It's just right!" And she ate everything in the **tazón**. "*Gracias!*" she said to the

empty **tazón**. Well, now she was even more **cansada** than ever after eating so much food. So, she decided to rest. In the living room, she saw a chair...but not just

silla

uno, not just **dos**, but **tres**! **Uno**, **dos**, **tres**! So, she sat down in the **silla** of the **papá oso**, which was very *grande*, and said, "Oh! This **silla** is definitely too

hard!" Then she sat in the **silla** that belonged to the **mamá** and said, "Oh! This **silla** is too soft!" Then she sat in the **silla** of the **pequeño bebé oso** and said,

→ **dura**

→ **blanda**

15

"Ahhh. This **silla** isn't too **dura**. It isn't too **blanda**. It's just right!" But just as she got comfortable... *Crack!* The **silla** of the **pequeño bebé oso** completely fell apart!

Still **cansada**, she decided to look for the bedroom to take a little nap. In front of her, she saw a bed ...but not just **uno**, not just **dos**, but **tres**! **Uno, dos, tres**!

cama

So, she tried the **cama** of the **papá oso** and said, "This **cama** is too **dura**!" Then she tried the **cama** that belonged to the **mamá** and said, "This **cama** is too **blanda**!"

Then she tried the **cama** of the **pequeño bebé oso** and said, "Ahhh. This **cama** isn't too **dura**. It isn't too **blanda**. It's just right!" And she fell fast asleep.

At that very **momento**, the **oso** family returned from their **paseo**. But upon entering the **casa**, the **papá oso** noticed something. "Someone's been eating my soup!" he said.

"And someone's been eating my soup!" said the **mamá** who was very confused. "And someone's been eating MY soup and ate it all up!" cried the **pequeño bebé oso**.

The **papá oso** walked into the living room and was very surprised at what he saw. "Look!" he said angrily. "Someone's been sitting in my **silla**!"

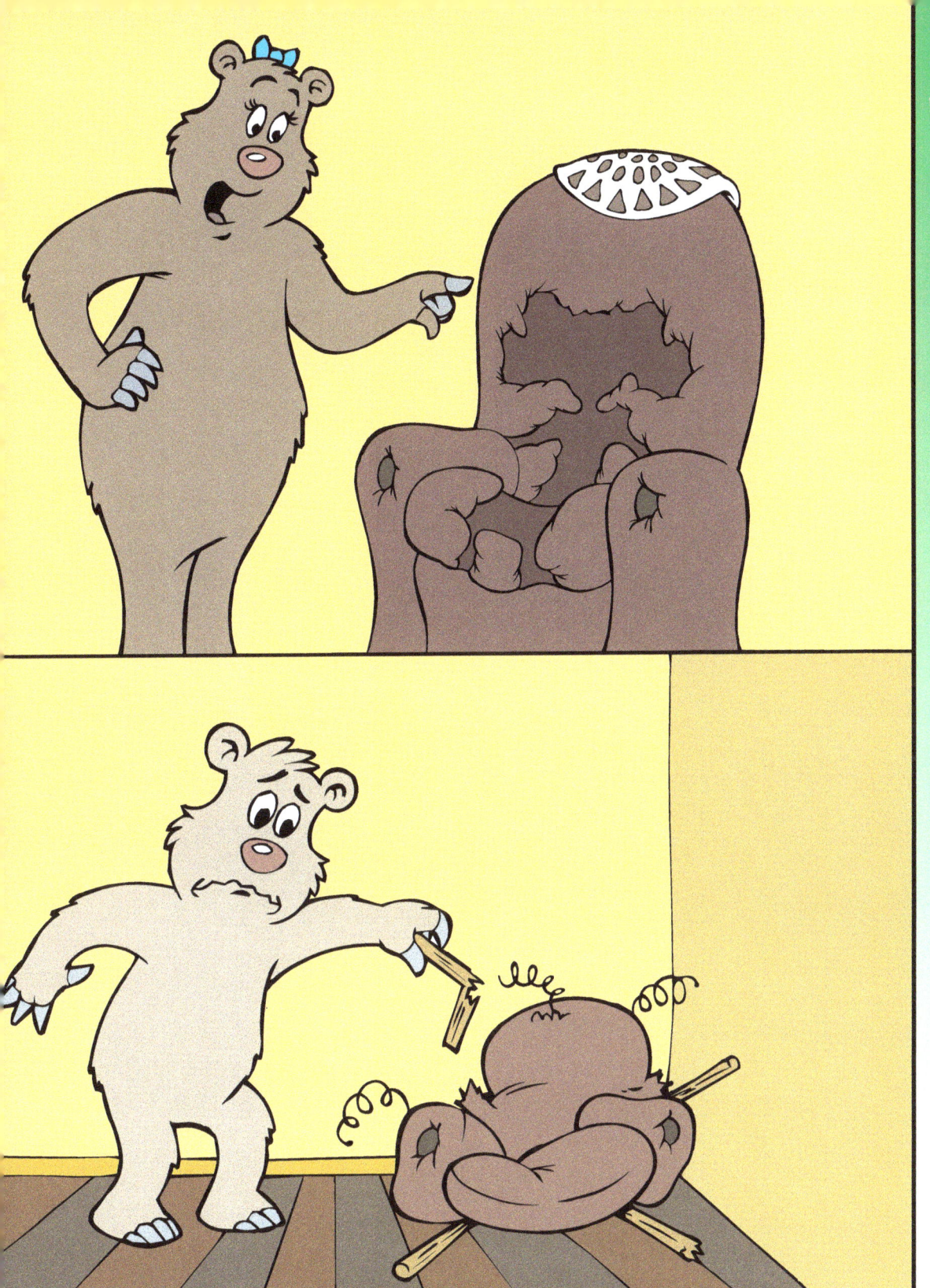

"And someone's been sitting in my **silla**!" said the **mamá**. "And someone's been sitting in MY **silla** and broke it into pieces!" cried the poor **pequeño bebé oso**.

Then the **oso** family heard snoring coming from the bedroom, so they went in to look. Something wasn't right. "Someone's been sleeping in my **cama**!" said the **papá oso**.

"And someone's been sleeping in my **cama**" said the surprised **mamá**. "And someone's been sleeping in MY **cama** and there she is!" shouted the **pequeño bebé oso**.

25

At that very **momento**, Goldilocks woke up and saw the entire **oso** family! The **oso** family thought the young **muchacha** was very **mala** to use their **casa** without

permission! "Oh, *gracias!*" she said to the **papá oso**. "*Gracias* for letting me eat food from your **tazón**, sit in your **silla**, and lie in your **cama**! *Gracias!*"

she said again, expecting the **oso** family to say, "*De nada!*" But they were angry that she caused so much trouble in their *casa* and the **oso** family growled at her.

So, she slowly stood up on the **cama** of the **pequeño bebé oso**, and said nervously, "Well, *gracias* for having me and… *Adiós!*" And with that, Goldilocks jumped off the **cama**, and dashed out the front **puerta**, running as fast as each *pie* could move. Needless to say, she never returned to visit the *casa* of the **oso** family again!

Level 3 contains words from Levels 1 & 2, plus all NEW words!

For more HEY WORDY! products, visit...